WORLDS OF THE PAST
THE ROMANS

Jacqueline Dineen

new
Discovery
B·O·O·K·S
New York

First New Discovery Books edition 1992

Originally published by
HEINEMANN CHILDREN'S REFERENCE
a division of Heinemann Educational Books Ltd
Halley Court, Jordan Hill, Oxford OX2 8EJ

OXFORD LONDON EDINBURGH
MELBOURNE SYDNEY AUCKLAND
MADRID ATHENS BOLOGNA
SINGAPORE IBADAN NAIROBI HARARE
GABORONE KINGSTON PORTSMOUTH NH(USA)

© Heinemann Educational Books Ltd 1991
First published 1991

Designed by Julian Holland Publishing Ltd
Color artwork by Martin Smillie
Picture research by Faith Perkins
Editorial planning by Jackie Gaff

New Discovery Books
Macmillan Publishing Company
866 Third Avenue
New York, NY 10022

Macmillan Publishing Company is part of the
Maxwell Communication Group of Companies.

Printed in Hong Kong

First Edition
10 9 8 7 6 5 4 3 2 1

Library of Congress Cataloging-in-Publication Data
Dineen, Jacqueline.
    The Romans / Jacqueline Dineen
        p.   cm. — (Worlds of the Past)
    Includes index.
    Summary: Surveys the history and civilization of Rome,
including views of government, law, social life and customs,
architecture, and religion.
    ISBN 0-02-730651-8
    1. Rome — Civilization — Juvenile literature. [1. Rome —
Civilization.] I. Title. II. Series.
DG77.D59   1992
937 — dc20   91 – 511

Photographic acknowledgments
The author and publisher wish to acknowledge, with
thanks, the following photographic sources:
a = above b = below l = left r = right
R. Agache p24; Ancient Art and Architecture Collection
pp5a and cover, 6a, 8l and r, 9a, 12b, 13 and cover, 14b,
19, 21, 22a, 23a, 30, 33r, 35a, 38l, 40, 42, 45a and b, 49, 50r,
51, 52b, 55, 56a, 59; British Museum p16l; C M Dixon
pp5b, 10, 26a, 31l, 35b; Sonia Halliday Photographs
pp6b; 38r; Michael Holford title page, pp7 and cover,
14a, 15, 16r, 23b, 31r and l, 36, 39, 41, 43a and b, 46, 47, 48,
54, 56b, 57, 58; Hulton Picture Company p52a; Museum of
London, photographs Jan Sorivener pp9b, 34; Mansell
Collection pp12a, 17, 20, 50l; Picturepoint p28; Scala p18;
Trustees of the National Museums of Scotland p27; Reg
Wilson p53.
The publishers have made every effort to trace the
copyright holders but if they have inadvertently
overlooked any, they will be pleased to make the
necessary arrangement at the first opportunity.

Note to the reader
In this book there are some words in the text which are printed in **bold** type. This shows that the word is listed in
the glossary on page 62. The glossary gives a brief explanation of words which may be new to you.

Contents

Who were the Romans? 4
How we know about the Romans 6
Evidence in words and pictures 8
Government 10
Society and the law 12
Clothes and appearance 14
Family life 16
Going to school 18
Gods and goddesses 20
Temples and shrines 22
A farm estate 24
The farming year 26
A town in the empire 28
Builders 30
Inside a town house 32
Cooking and eating 34
At the baths 36
A public holiday 38
Crafts and trades 40
Shopkeepers 42
Trade and transport 44
Expansion and conquest 46
Legionaries and centurions 48
At war 50
Wars in Italy 52
The emperors 54
A Roman province 56
The fall of Rome 58
Time line 60
Glossary 62
Index 64

Who were the Romans?

Between 2000 and 1000 B.C. groups of people from central Asia began moving into the country we now call Italy. They spoke different languages. One group, whose language was called Latin, settled on the south bank of the Tiber River. Their settlement was surrounded by seven small hills that protected the people from **invaders**. The Latins farmed the flat land by the river and began to trade with other settlers. They built villages on the hilltops. In time these villages became the city of Rome.

After a while the people of Rome began to quarrel over who should be leader. When Ancus Marcius, who built the first bridge over the Tiber, died in 616 B.C., the Romans chose an Etruscan as their next king. The Etruscans were a group of people who had settled in northern Italy and gradually **conquered** most of the country. They passed their knowledge of building, metalwork, and sculpture to the Romans. The seventh Etruscan king, Tarquinius the Proud, was harsh and unpopular. The Romans rebelled and drove Tarquinius and the Etruscans out. They

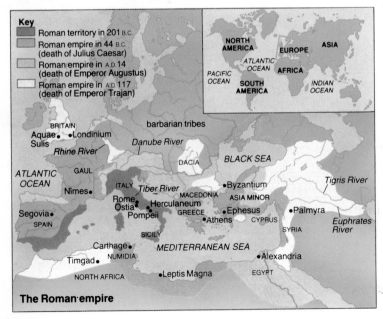

The Roman empire

Key
- Roman territory in 201 B.C.
- Roman empire in 44 B.C. (death of Julius Caesar)
- Roman empire in A.D. 14 (death of Emperor Augustus)
- Roman empire in A.D. 117 (death of Emperor Trajan)

B.C. and A.D.
Each year has a number. These numbers, or dates, record when things happen. Dates are measured from the year when Jesus Christ was born. Any date before the birth of Christ is called B.C. The date is written with the letters after the number (2 B.C.). Remember that 1 B.C. is more recent than 2 B.C. Dates since the birth of Christ have the letters A.D. They stand for Anno Domini. These Latin words mean "in the year of the Lord." So A.D. 1 means "in the first year of the life of Christ, the Lord." The letters A.D. always come before the date (A.D. 1, A.D. 2).

The Romans divided their year into months to match changes in the moon. Their year only had 355 days (12 new moons), so the months got out of step with the seasons. Julius Caesar introduced a new calendar, based on the sun. It had 365 days with a leap year, as we have today. The Earth takes just over 365 days to go around the sun.

◁ Roman roads, bridges, and buildings can still be seen today. The Colosseum in Rome was completed in A.D. 80. It was 170 feet (52 m) high and held 50,000 people. The Romans used rows of arches to support the walls. They built the arch around a semicircular wooden frame and put in the top, or keystone, last. When the frame was removed, the stones on either side pressed against the keystone and made a strong support.

decided they would not have another king and set up a **republic**. The leader of the republic was chosen by the people for a fixed length of time. At the end of that time, they could choose a new leader.

Rome was a republic for nearly 500 years. During that time the Romans became powerful and conquered many other lands, including Greece. Then once again Rome was ruled by one powerful man. In 27 B.C., Gaius Julius Caesar Octavius was given the name Augustus which means "great." He was also given the power of an **emperor** and ruled not just Rome but also all the lands conquered by the Romans. At this time the Roman **empire** included 60 million people.

Rome was the center of this empire for 300 years. Latin was spoken in all the lands the Romans ruled and remains the basis of many other languages today including English. The Romans also spread their skills in building and their knowledge of science throughout the empire.

△ The Romans learned a lot about art from the Greeks. They admired the beauty of Greek statues. This wall painting, from a house in the town of Pompeii in Italy, is nearly 2,000 years old. The painting may show the owner of the house and his wife. The painting is now in a museum in Naples.

How we know about the Romans

We know a great deal about the Roman **civilization**, or way of life. There is evidence in the finds of **archaeologists**. They dig down, or **excavate**, to find remains buried under the earth. Archaeologists may find pottery, jewelry and household items that tell them more about how people lived. Sometimes they find graves containing objects that were buried with the dead. These give us clues about religious beliefs. Archaeologists may find old buildings or even whole towns and cities.

Sometimes clues are discovered by accident, by builders or by people building roads. In 1709 people digging a well in Italy found an **amphitheater** — the outdoor theater of Herculaneum. A few years later, farmers plowing the fields discovered the site of nearby Pompeii. Both these cities had been destroyed in A.D. 79 when the volcano of

△ Archaeologists uncover every find very carefully. They may discover pieces of pottery that can be put together. They sift through the soil so that they do not miss small objects like coins, hairpins, and pieces of jewelry.

◁ Some Roman buildings can still be seen because people did not build over the same place. This is Palmyra, the ancient "city of palm trees" in the desert of Syria. An oasis provided water for travelers. The Romans added new buildings to the city in the 1st century A.D. It was destroyed 200 years later by the Roman emperor Aurelian because the people of Palmyra had become too powerful. No one lived there again.

The Romans had a legend about how Rome was founded. Roman writers such as Livy and Virgil developed the story, but it may have been started by the Greek historian Hellanicus in the 5th century B.C.

The story began when the Greeks captured the city of Troy in Asia Minor. A Trojan hero named Aeneas escaped and sailed to Italy. He founded a kingdom on the plain of Latium, the land farmed by the Latins. A descendant of Aeneas, King Numitor, was driven out by his wicked brother. Numitor had twin grandsons, Romulus and Remus. His brother had the babies thrown into the Tiber River. The cradle was washed ashore and the babies were cared for by a she-wolf, until they were found by a shepherd who brought them up.

When the twins grew up, they decided to build a city at the place where they had been rescued. As they began to build the walls, the brothers quareled and Romulus killed Remus. The legend said that Rome was built in 753 B.C. and named after Romulus who was its first king.

Mount Vesuvius erupted. Thousands of people were killed. The city of Pompeii was buried under hot ash and Herculaneum was buried under mud washed down from the volcano by rain. An archaeologist called Giuseppe Fiorelli organized careful digging at Pompeii from 1860 to 1875.

Archaeologists also study old documents and try to piece together the history. In the 1970s American archaeologists found the Roman seaside town of Kourion on the island of Cyprus. It had been badly damaged by an earthquake in A.D. 342. A Syrian historian, Ammianus Marcellinus, saw the disaster and wrote about it. The archaeologists followed up these written clues and found the ancient port.

Evidence in words and pictures

The Romans wrote letters and books about their daily life and their history. Many have survived in libraries. They tell us in great detail about how the Romans lived. The historian Livy wrote 142 books on the history of Rome. Another historian called Tacitus lived 100 years later, from A.D. 55 to 120. He wrote about what happened in his own lifetime. Tacitus was a great friend of the writer Pliny, who wrote many letters to friends about his home and his daily life. Pliny's uncle wrote the *Historia Naturalis*, a series of books that include descriptions of paintings, statues, and buildings, as well as scientific discoveries. He lived near Mount Vesuvius and was killed when the volcano erupted in A.D. 79. The younger Pliny wrote about the eruption and how his uncle died.

Other clues

Other words tell us about Roman life. They are not in books but carved on stone or scribbled on walls. Archaeologists found graffiti in Pompeii. People wrote on walls then, just as they do today. Some graffiti referred to elections of town officials. "Julius Philippus, vote for him and he'll do the same for you."

◁ Some fragments of writing on papyrus, a type of paper made from a plant, have been found. They are not always easy to read.

▷ Words carved on stone are much clearer. Inscriptions on tombs usually praise the dead person. The tombstone in the picture shows a Roman cavalryman fighting bravely for the empire.

Latin

Latin was the official language of the Roman empire. The conquered countries of the empire had their own languages, but people were expected to speak and read Latin as well. Latin has survived because it became the official language of the Christian Church. Priests continued to write in Latin. Church libraries kept copies of Roman literature. The writings of Virgil became models of the best use of Latin in his own lifetime. His books have been studied in schools ever since.

△ This stone carving gives us information about Roman clothes and hairstyles. A lady is having her hair done by a maid. Other maids are holding pots of scented oils. One maid holds a metal mirror. Archaeologists may often find pieces of pottery and metal, and pictures like this show them how these things were used.

Someone wrote, "I wonder, wall, that you have not yet collapsed under the weight of the idiocies with which these imbeciles have covered you."

Stone carvings, or **inscriptions**, record the names of builders. Inscriptions on tombs tell us about the dead people. Important items like documents and certificates were inscribed on bronze and many of these have been found by archaeologists.

Wall paintings give us many details about everyday life in the Roman empire. Sculptures and carvings show us what people looked like. Many statues of important Romans were set up in temples, libraries, and city streets.

◁ Mosaic floors were laid by a team of workmen under the instructions of a designer. The mosaics were made from cubes of colored stone or glass. When buildings fell into disuse, they were often pulled down and a new building put up. Many mosaic floors were buried under these new buildings, which protected them. Archaeologists have uncovered many fine examples, which supply more evidence about Roman life.

Government

When Rome became a republic, the people were determined that no one person should have too much power. The Latin words *res publica* mean "the thing belonging to everybody." However, the people of Rome were not all equals. Women, slaves, and people who were not born in Rome were not considered **citizens**. Therefore they could not vote to choose their leaders.

The citizens of Rome met in a group called a *comitia,* or an assembly. There were four assemblies in Rome. Officials were elected by the assemblies once a year. These officials were all **magistrates**, which means they had power to enforce the law. The names of the magistrates were written on a board in the **forum**, the central meeting place in Rome.

The most powerful magistrates were the two **consuls**. They had to agree with each other because one consul could cancel, or veto, the other's decision. The assemblies also elected four other types of magistrates. *Quaestores* looked after the city's money. *Aediles* were in charge of public buildings. *Censors* kept records of all the people and worked out how much tax everybody had to pay. The two

▷ The forum was an open market square or meeting place. The Forum Romanum became the center of government in Rome. Buildings were added around each side.

The first *curia,* or senate house, was built about 670 B.C. This is where the senators met to discuss problems. Between 184 and 169 B.C., three *basilicas* or large halls were built. These were used for business meetings, and law courts. Politicians spoke to the people from a large outdoor platform, or *rostra.* After a battle at sea in 338 B.C., the front, or *rostra,* of an enemy ship was brought here and gave the platform its name. Cicero, a writer and statesman, was murdered in 43 B.C. and his head and hands were displayed on the *rostra* where he had made his famous speeches.

◁ The Forum Romanum was also a center of religion, with temples and shrines. The columns of the Temple of Castor and Pollux still stand. These gods were worshiped in Rome because people believed they had helped the Romans in a battle.

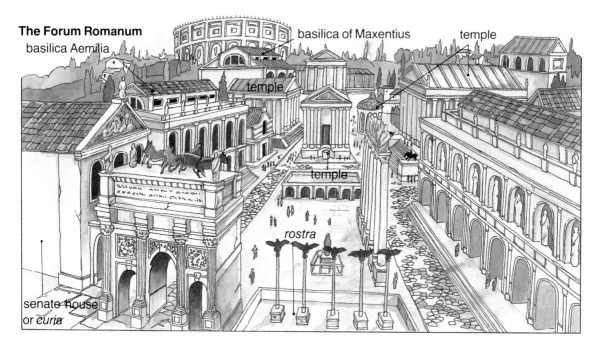

The Forum Romanum
basilica Aemilia
basilica of Maxentius
temple
temple
temple
rostra
senate house
or *curia*

praetors were the chief judges. One was in charge of
the trials of Romans, while the other dealt with
foreigners.

After a year, most magistrates became members of
the **senate** for the rest of their lives. During the
republic the consuls and the *censors* chose people to
join the senate. At different times there were between
300 and 900 members and it was their job to advise the
consuls.

The system of government changed when Julius
Caesar became **dictator** in 45 B.C. He was a strong
military commander who was not elected but took
control. From 27 B.C., the emperor chose the
members of the senate himself. He also decided who
would be the next emperor.

Each Roman territory, or **province**, was ruled by a
governor, in the name of the people of Rome. The
senate, and later the emperor, chose the governors,
who had usually been magistrates in Rome.

Society and the law

Roman citizens were divided into two classes. The **patricians** were rich nobles who owned a lot of land. The **plebeians** were tradesmen, servants, and men with small farms. There were many more plebeians than patricians but only the patricians could become magistrates and members of the senate. The patricians also had more votes than the plebeians. Rome was supposed to be a **democracy**, but the plebeians did not have equal rights. Rome was really run by the patricians.

In 494 B.C., the plebeians who felt bitter about the system of government threatened to leave Rome and set up a rival city nearby. This threat worried the patricians because they needed workers in the city. Finally they agreed that the plebeians could choose two officers called **tribunes**. These officers could not make laws but they would veto the actions of the patrician magistrates or consuls. Before long,

△ Slaves worked for nothing and were often harshly treated by their masters. Many worked in mines or on farms. Life was easier for household slaves. Greek slaves were well educated and often became secretaries and tutors. Slaves had no legal rights and were not allowed to vote. Some slaves were freed when their masters died. They became *libertini,* or freedmen. The freedmen in this carving are Demetrius and Philonicus, freed slaves of Publius Licinius. They worked as carpenters. Their tools are also shown on the carving.

◁ Citizens who wanted to be elected as magistrates in the republic had to win the popularity of the people. Rich patricians did this by offering free entertainment for the poor people. The writing on this wall in Pompeii advertises public fights paid for by a wealthy man called Lucretius Satrus. He asks people to vote for Quintus Postumus.

plebeians were allowed to become magistrates and members of the senate. The first plebeian consul, Licinius, was elected in 366 B.C. From that time, one consul was always a plebeian.

Roman law

For many years the laws of the city were kept secret by the magistrates. People began to complain. In about 450 B.C., the laws of Rome, with punishments for certain crimes, were set out on twelve bronze tablets and put in the forum for everyone to see.

Any citizen could take a complaint to the law courts. Gaius Verres, governor of Sicily from 73 to 70 B.C., was accused of stealing treasures from houses and temples. Cicero spoke for the people of Sicily at the trial in Rome and won the case.

Over hundreds of years, new laws were made. In the 6th century, the laws of ancient Rome were collected together in a Code of Law by the emperor Justinian. Today many countries base their laws on the laws of ancient Rome.

Cicero

Most of the important men in Rome were lawyers or politicians. They won support from people by clever speeches. Marcus Tullius Cicero, who lived from 106 to 43 B.C., was a famous orator. His family was wealthy and came from Arpinum in southern Italy. By 70 B.C. Cicero had become Rome's leading lawyer. He was made a consul in 63 B.C.

Cicero wrote many speeches and letters in which he discussed the society and politics of ancient Rome. Over 900 of his letters survive. He translated the works of Greek philosophers into Latin and also wrote some books of his own. He admitted that many of his ideas came from the Greeks. His writings were used as textbooks at grammar schools and teachers of public speaking gave their pupils his speeches as examples to follow. His speeches and letters are also fine examples of Latin prose.

Clothes and appearance

Wall paintings, mosaics, and statues of Romans show clearly the type of clothes they wore. Their clothes were loose and simple, usually made of one piece of fabric.

Men wore a knee-length tunic with short sleeves. The tunic was held in by a belt at the waist. Roman citizens wore **togas** over their tunics. A toga was like a long sheet that was wound around the body, over the left shoulder and under the right arm. Togas were cumbersome but the Romans were proud of them because only citizens were allowed to wear them.

Women wore a long tunic with another tunic, called a **stola**, on top. The stola was fastened on the shoulders or down the arms with brooches called fibulae. When women went out, they also wore cloaks called pallas, which could be wrapped around their heads. Children's clothes were very like their parents'. Boys wore short tunics with cloaks. Girls wore ankle-length tunics with shawls or cloaks.

Most clothes worn by the Romans were made of wool. The wool came from sheep that archaeologists know once grazed all over Italy. Richer people could

△ As the Romans conquered more lands and became more prosperous, they began to wear more jewelry. They copied the Greek design of a snake for bracelets. Archaeologists have found necklaces, gold rings, and hairpins. The gold came from Spain and the precious stones came from Asia. Earrings show that Roman women had pierced ears. Children wore amulets, little charms that people believed would keep them safe. Men had signet rings. They used the picture on the ring to make a mark in wax on their letters.

◁ Statues give us clear evidence about clothes and how they were draped. Men often wore brooches to hold their togas in place. The emperors gave inscribed brooches to leaders of their armies.

▷ Men and women wore sandals at home and soft leather boots when they went out. Poor people and slaves went barefoot.

buy finer linen or silk. The linen was made from a plant called flax which did not grow in Italy. This made the fabric expensive because the Romans had to buy it from Egypt. Silk had to be brought from China by traders.

Hairstyles

Rich women had slaves to do their hair for them, so their hairstyles were very elaborate. The hair was curled and piled up into different styles. Some women liked to dye their hair blonde, because dark hair was more common in Rome. The dye came from Mainz, which is now part of Germany. Blonde wigs or hairpieces were bought from other countries. Men's hairstyles often followed the style of the emperor. When an emperor like Hadrian had a beard other men grew beards too.

Family life

Family and home were very important to the Romans. The Latin word *familia* meant more than just father, mother, and children. A Roman family included slaves and servants who were paid for their work, as well as grandparents, unmarried aunts and uncles, and the household gods. The father had total control over everyone else. Cicero wrote that a senator called Fluvius ordered the death of his own son for disobedience. If a newborn baby was weak or ill, the father might decide to allow it to die.

Weddings

Fathers arranged marriages for their children. Girls were often married when they were only 13, and boys were not much older. A lawyer called Ulpianus, who lived from A.D. 170 to 228, wrote about the marriage ceremony. At the bride's home, the fathers signed a marriage contract. Prayers and a special cake were offered to the gods and goddesses. As the bride and bridegroom joined hands, the bride said the words, *"Ubi tu Gaius, ego Gaia,"* which mean "Where you are master, I am mistress." After a feast, the bride was

◁△ This gold wedding ring and the stone carving show the joining of hands which was part of the wedding ceremony. A Roman bride wore a wedding ring on the third finger of her left hand, as many married women do today. Her dress was white and she wore an orange shawl over her head, like the flames of torches in the wedding procession. Wall paintings show the colors of clothes.

taken in a torchlight procession to the bridegroom's house. He carried her over the entrance, or threshold, of her new home. This was done so the bride would not trip at the entrance. If she did it would bring bad luck. The Roman writer Plautus describes a wedding feast in his play *Aulularia,* which means "Pot of Gold." In the play the bride's father is a mean man who hates having to spend his money on food for the wedding feast.

Roman women were expected to obey their husbands but they could keep their own property. Pliny's letters to his wife show she was a good companion and helped him with his work. If a couple did not want to live together anymore they could divorce.

Roman names

When a baby was a few days old, it was presented to the father at a special ceremony. If he took the baby in his arms, the child was named and given a locket, called a *bulla*.

A child was given three names. The first was a personal name, like Marcus. Then came the name of the clan, or group of families. Tullius meant "one of the Tullius clan." The last name was the particular family's name, like Cicero, or Caesar.

▽ The carving shows a boy's life between babyhood and his first lessons from his father. The father watches as the child is fed. Then he holds him to show he accepts the baby. The little boy plays in a toy cart drawn by a donkey. Other pictures show dogs, and even geese, pulling children's carts. Children also had hoops, dice, and dolls.

Going to school

The Romans thought children learned the most important things at home. Parents taught their children to obey rules, to tell the truth, and to help other people. Varro wrote in one of his 600 books that parents kept their children with them all the time. When the family had visitors children stayed up late so they could listen to the adults talking.

Education began to change when the Romans conquered the Greeks and began to study Greek literature. A Greek named Livius Andronicus came to Rome as a prisoner of war in 272 B.C. He translated the works of the Greek poet Homer into Latin. Some Romans bought Greek slaves to teach their children. Cato thought the education of his son was too important to leave to a slave. He wrote a book describing how he taught his son at home.

Teachers began to set up schools where children

◁ The daughters of wealthy families sometimes continued their education after elementary school. Writers joked about well-educated women. Juvenal said that he loathed women who kept quoting Homer and Virgil. The girl in this wall painting is writing on a wooden board covered with wax. She scratches the letters into the wax with a stylus.

◁ Many Roman children had their lessons at home. These boys are wearing outdoor shoes and warm clothes to go to school. They are reading from papyrus scrolls. The teacher is looking crossly at the boy who is late. Parents had to pay fees for schools, so only children from rich families went.

could go when they were seven. A teacher named Quintilian wrote a book about education, *Institutio Oratoria,* which gives us valuable information about schools in Rome.

The children learned to read and write in Latin and Greek. They wrote with a pointed instrument called a **stylus** and learned to count with rows of beads on an **abacus**.

Girls normally left school at 13. Boys went on to a secondary school, or *grammaticus,* where they learned about the art of public speaking, or **oratory**. Boys also studied Greek and Roman literature. Slaves helped to copy the works of poets such as Homer and Virgil onto sheets of rough paper, called papyrus. The sheets were then glued and rolled to make books.

Boys left school at 16. When their beards first grew, they went through a special ceremony to show that they had reached manhood. Toys and children's clothes were put aside, and the boy put on a *toga virilis.* This showed that he was a man and a citizen of Rome.

After school, boys of rich parents could go to Athens to study law and oratory, or to study with Greek thinkers, or **philosophers**. Poorer boys became **apprentices** to learn a trade or craft.

Roman numerals
The Romans used a system of letters for their numerals. You still see these today as dates on tombstones and statues and often as the numbers on clocks.

In the Roman system, I = 1, V = 5, X = 10, L = 50, C = 100, D = 500, and M = 1000. Numbers in between were written as additions or subtractions. For example, 4 could be written as IIII or IV. IV means 5 – 1. VI means 5 +1, or 6. This system was difficult for children to work with because numbers could become very long and unwieldy. Imagine trying to multiply or divide using these numbers!

Gods and goddesses

The Romans believed in many gods and goddesses. They believed that the gods were all around them and influenced everything they did. Most of the gods were the same as the gods worshiped by the Greeks, but the Romans called them by different names.

The Romans believed that if they pleased the gods, the gods would bring them luck. When they died, they believed that the god Mercury led the spirits of the dead to a river that divided the world of the living from the **underworld**. There, the spirits crossed to this other land which was ruled over by a god and goddess.

By the first century B.C., many people had begun to lose faith in the old gods. They began to adopt gods from other lands. In Egypt they found that people worshiped Isis, the mother goddess who promised life after death. Soldiers were attracted to the Persian sun-god, Mithras, who was supposed to give courage. The Romans conquered many people and were prepared to accept the religions, or **cults**, of most of them. One exception was the Druid cult that they found in Britain. The Druid priests sacrificed people and animals during their rituals. The Romans

▽ A funeral for the dead was very important. A dead person's soul could not rest in the underworld unless the correct ceremony was held. Burial grounds were outside towns. This tomb carving shows the procession of mourners and musicians that took the body there. Sometimes the dead were burned, or cremated, with all their possessions. Families remembered their dead at special festivals during the year.

would not let people follow this religion.

When the first emperor, Augustus, died in A.D. 14, the senate said Augustus was now a god. People were expected to worship his statue on festival days.

Jesus Christ was born during the reign of Augustus. The Romans would not accept Christ or his Christian followers because they refused to worship the emperor. Thousands of Christians were killed or imprisoned for their beliefs. Even so, Christianity eventually spread throughout the empire. Many people admired the courage and goodness of the Christians. Nearly 300 years after the death of Jesus Christ, the emperor Constantine became a Christian. He made Christianity the official religion of the Roman empire.

△ The gods shown from left to right on this stone carving are Hercules, Minerva, Bacchus, Jupiter, Ceres, Juno, and Mercury.

The Roman gods

(Greek name in brackets)
Jupiter *(Zeus):* god of the sky and king of all the gods. His temple stood on Capitoline Hill in Rome.
Juno *(Hera):* wife of Jupiter, goddess of women and mothers.
The Romans believed that the other gods were members of Jupiter and Juno's family. These included:
Mars *(Ares):* god of war.
Ceres *(Demeter):* goddess of farming.
Venus *(Aphrodite):* goddess of love and beauty.
Minerva *(Athena):* goddess of crafts and wisdom.
Mercury *(Hermes):* messenger of the gods; god of trade.
Diana *(Artemis):* goddess of the moon and of hunting.
Neptune *(Poseidon):* god of the sea.
Vulcan *(Hephaistos):* god of fire; the blacksmith.
Vesta *(Hestia):* goddess of the hearth.
Bacchus *(Dionysos):* god of wine.
Saturn *(Kronos):* god of farming and weights and measures.
Janus *(no Greek equivalent):* god of doorways and journeys.
Apollo: Greek god of light, music and the arts. *(The Romans did not change his name.)*

Temples and shrines

The Romans built temples to all their different gods, but the people did not go into a temple to pray. They thought of the temple as the home of the god or goddess. Inside, there was a **shrine** with a statue of the god or goddess. Each temple had priests or priestesses who made offerings to the gods. The Romans thought that they could please the gods best by giving them gifts of food or treasures. On festival days, animals were sacrificed outside the temples. Each occasion had a very strict pattern of words and actions. It was important to get everything exactly right, or the gods would be displeased.

Priests also looked for signs or omens from the gods. Thunder and lightning were bad omens. The Romans never did anything important if the omens were bad. They also liked to look into the future. Some people consulted religious officials, called **augurs**, who told the future by watching the flight of birds. Other people went to astrologers who worked out events in a person's life by studying the arrangement of the stars. Astrologers and augurs charged high fees, so poor people went to the cheaper soothsayers. One type, a *haruspex*, used a dove to tell fortunes, while a *conjectores* told the

△ The Romans borrowed many of their ideas about architecture from the Greeks. Like Greek temples, this temple has a roof supported by columns. It is at Nimes, in France, which was part of the Roman empire. The temple is very well preserved. It was built in 16 B.C. to honor Garius and Lucius Caesar, grandsons of the Emperor Augustus.

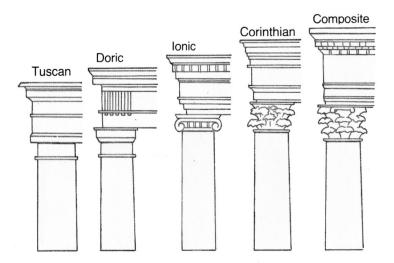

Tuscan Doric Ionic Corinthian Composite

◁ The Romans used five sorts of columns. Three of these were adapted from Greek architecture. The Doric column was fairly plain. The Ionic style had carvings at the top. The Corinthian column was the most elaborate and was used on the temple at Nimes. The Romans also used a plain Tuscan column, and a Composite column, which combined styles.

meaning of dreams. Cicero, Pliny the Elder, and Tacitus all wrote about fortune-telling. Tacitus felt there was some truth in the stories he recorded. Cicero and Pliny did not believe in signs or omens.

The Romans also believed in household gods. These spirits helped the Romans in their daily lives. The *lares* protected the home and the family while the *penates* had control of the store cupboard. The family prayed to the *penates* to provide enough food. Vesta was the spirit of the hearth, or fire. There were altars to the household gods in every home.

△ Small statues of the household gods were placed on an altar in front of the hearth in the living room or in the courtyard of a Roman house. Examples have been found at Pompeii and many other Roman towns. People prayed to the household gods as soon as they got up in the morning and whenever they left or entered the house. Every morning and evening they made offerings of flowers and wine to the gods as this family is doing on the stone carving.

Medicine and healing

Many Romans thought illness was a punishment by the gods. They made sacrifices so the gods would cure an illness. From the Greeks, they began to learn about medicine. Archaeologists have found medical instruments like those in the picture as well as stone carvings showing doctors at work. Eye infections were a common problem and one carving shows an eye doctor treating a patient. Doctors sold ointments made from herbs which were supposed to cure eye troubles. Pliny writes about a mustard gargle which was good for stomach upsets. Roman doctors charged high fees. Before going to the doctor, people often tried to buy a cure from a druggist.

A farm estate

In early times, most Romans were farmers. Each family farmed a small plot of land to grow their own food. However, long years of wars ruined many families. The men had to go away and fight. Many of them died leaving nobody to work on the land. Some of the land was given as a reward to commanders in the army. Prisoners were also brought back to Rome to work as slaves.

By 100 B.C., nearly all farming was done on large estates. We know how these estates were laid out and run from archaeological finds and also from Roman

▽ Aerial views show archaeologists the layouts of ruined Roman buildings or towns now under farmers' fields. If the owner of the land does not mind, archaeologists can then excavate the site. The drawing shows what archaeologists think a Roman country estate at Estrees-sur-Noye in northern France looked like. The photograph is an aerial view of the site.

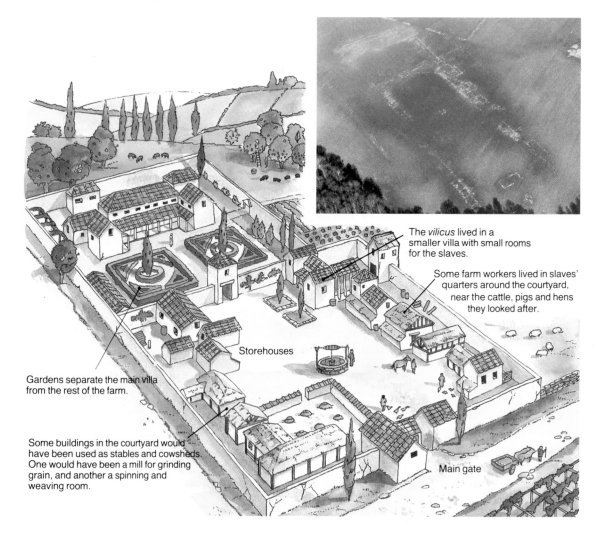

The *vilicus* lived in a smaller villa with small rooms for the slaves.

Some farm workers lived in slaves' quarters around the courtyard, near the cattle, pigs and hens they looked after.

Storehouses

Gardens separate the main villa from the rest of the farm.

Some buildings in the courtyard would have been used as stables and cowsheds. One would have been a mill for grinding grain, and another a spinning and weaving room.

Main gate

writers. One of these writers, Lucius Columella, wrote a book called *About Farming* in A.D. 60. Columella was not a Roman. He came from southern Spain and settled near Rome to farm. Virgil came from a farming family and we can learn about farming methods from his poem, *The Georgics*.

The wealthy owners of the farm estates lived in the cities for most of the year. They visited their farms in the summer, when the heat made the city life unpleasant. The owners stayed in a large villa on the estate. The farm was run by a farm manager called a *vilicus* and a housekeeper, the *vilica*. The farm work was done by slaves.

Buildings and plants

Archaeologists have found Roman farm sites throughout Europe and in North Africa. From pieces of stone, brick, and tiles, archaeologists can tell what the buildings looked like. They know which crops were grown from seeds, nuts, and the remains of vegetables and cereals that they find in the soil. Different crops were grown in different parts of the empire, depending on the land and the climate.

The Romans planted crops in the lands they conquered, such as France and Britain. Many new plants, such as cabbages, carrots, cherries, and walnuts, were introduced into Britain by the Romans. Archaeologists have discovered that farms in Britain and northern France also grew wheat and barley and vegetables such as beans and peas, as well as plums, apples, and other fruit. Farmers in the north also grew clover to feed their animals.

The big estates had formal gardens near the villa. There were hedges and small trees of yew, box, and cypress. Plane trees were planted to give shade. Wall paintings show roses, lilies, and violets in Roman gardens.

The farming year

The farm estates of Rome could not provide sufficient food for people living in the cities. When the Roman army conquered lands, food was sent from these countries to Rome. The Romans imported grain from Sicily, North Africa, and Egypt. They exported wine to other parts of the empire. Some conquered lands, like Spain, had silver and gold mines. These made the Romans rich enough to buy goods from other countries.

Each part of the farming year had a special festival. The Romans offered gifts to the gods before plowing the land or sowing seed. Everyone on the farm took part in a special procession at the end of May, called the Ambarualia. They walked around the fields and asked the gods to help the crops to ripen. Races and a feast celebrated the end of the harvest in August.

Running the estate

An estate was like a small town. It provided everything the farm workers needed. The *vilicus* and

△ The Romans were fond of meat. Bones of pigs, goats, cows, and sheep have been found on the sites of farms. The Romans also hunted wild boar, deer, partridges, pheasants, and pigeons. This mosaic shows a boar hunt. The mosaic was found in Carthage in North Africa and dates from the 4th century A.D. The hunters are using a dog to chase the boar into a net. When they have caught the animal, they tie it to a long pole to bring it back to the estate.

◁ On Roman farms, enough grapes were grown to make wine for export to other countries. This mosaic shows grapes being picked and pressed to make wine. On the left, men are picking the fruit and loading it onto a cart. The grapes were taken to the farmyard, put into a stone trough, and crushed to squeeze out the juice. You can see this happening on the right. The juice was stored in jars and turned into wine. The pottery jars were half-buried in the ground to keep cool.

◁ These farm tools were found at Newstead, on the Tweed River in Scotland. The iron scythe on the left was used to cut wheat. There are two rakes. The rake on the right is made from the horns of a red deer. If a farm did not have its own blacksmith, the owner, or the *vilica*, hired a blacksmith from time to time to make tools.

vilica were slaves, but they had to be responsible and hardworking. Cato wrote of the *vilicus,* "He must be the first to rise in the morning and the last to bed." In between he had to supervise the other slaves on the farm and in the workshops. Slaves made cheese from cows' and goats' milk. Wool from sheep was spun and made into cloth by female slaves. Other slaves looked after chickens, ducks, and geese and collected honey from the beehives. Grain was threshed, or separated from the stalks, and ground into flour. Olives were pressed for oil that was used for cooking and lighting.

The Roman calendar
Until 46 B.C., the Roman year started on the first day of March. This is why September, October, November, and December mean seventh, eighth, ninth, and tenth months. Other months were named after gods or goddesses: January (Janus), March (Mars), May (Maia), June (Juno). February was from the name for a special ceremony. April meant "the opening of flowers." When Julius Caesar reorganized the calendar, he named July after himself. The emperor Augustus did the same with August.

A town in the empire

Archaeologists have found many examples of Roman cities all over the empire. In some of these, such as Bath in England, Nîmes in France, and Rome itself, Roman buildings are scattered among more modern ones. Other cities are still complete, just as they were when the Romans lived there. The cities of Timgad in Algeria and Volubilis in Morocco still stand in ruins. Visitors can see what the shops and houses were like, even how the drains and water pipes were laid. Many Roman ruins are still buried. In August 1988 floods uncovered marble columns in a village in Turkey. Archaeologists have found carvings there which show it was the city of Sebastopolis. The emperor Augustus founded this city in the year 2 B.C.

Roman towns were laid out on a grid system. This means that the streets were straight and crossed one

▽ Thamugadi, now called Timgad in Algeria, North Africa, was built in A.D. 100 as a colony for Roman soldiers. By the middle of the 2nd century, the town had expanded.

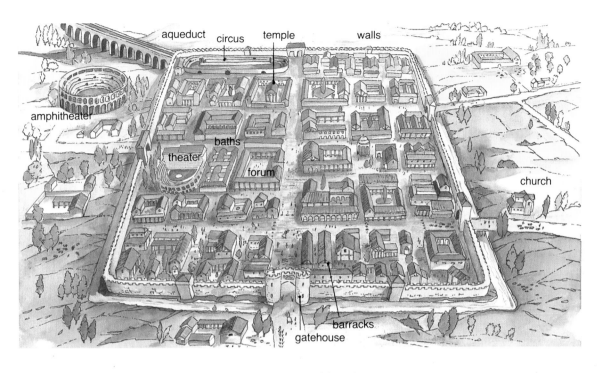

another at right angles. The Romans got this idea from the Greeks, who planned many of their towns in this way. The roads divided the towns into squares. The buildings on these squares were called *insulae,* which is Latin for "islands."

The Romans built **aqueducts** to carry clean water from rivers and lakes to the towns. The name aqueduct comes from the Latin words for "water," and "to carry." An aqueduct is a channel for carrying water on a bridge across a valley or underground in pipes. Over 200 Roman aqueducts can still be seen.

Many Roman towns in the empire started as military forts where the soldiers lived. They were surrounded by strong walls and ditches. Other towns began as a **colony**. Roman citizens were given money and help to build a new town in a conquered land. They took seeds with them, to plant and grow food. The families lived in the town but went to work each day in the fields nearby.

Builders

We know about Roman building techniques from writers such as Vitruvius, an architect who wrote a manual of architecture in the 1st century A.D. Another writer, Julius Frontinus, was in charge of the water supply for Rome in A.D. 97. His books describe how water reached the public baths and fountains as well as people's houses.

Roman architects and engineers used arches to support their soaring aqueducts, bridges, and tall buildings. They realized that a semicircular shape that squeezed against a central keystone was the strongest shape to carry the weight of a wall or roof. The materials the builders used were stone, brick, and a form of **concrete** that they invented about 200 B.C.

◁ In A.D. 113 the Emperor Trajan dedicated a tall carved column to celebrate his military victories. The column records what happened. In the top row soldiers are building stone fortifications to protect them during the battle.

To carry out all their building projects, the Romans needed many workers. The buildings were planned and supervised by engineers and surveyors. Masons showed the workmen how to cut and lay the stones while slaves turned huge treadmills that lifted the blocks of stone to where they were needed. Engineers, surveyors, and masons from Rome went to work all over the empire. They taught their skills to other workers.

Roman roads

The Romans built a network of roads totaling 52,000 miles (85,000 km) to all parts of their empire. The roads were planned by surveyors traveling with the Roman army. First a surveyor studied the landscape to find the most direct route. Then soldiers and slaves dug a wide trench. The road was then built up in layers in the trench. These layers of sand, concrete, small stones, and stone blocks made the road very strong. The routes of the Roman roads are still part of the road system in Italy and other European countries today. This is because Roman roads were straight and took the shortest route from one place to the next.

△ In order to supply a town with water, the Romans looked for a source of water such as a river or lake that was higher than the town. Then engineers built the aqueduct so that it sloped gradually downhil. They lined the channel with concrete to stop the water leaking. The aqueducts usually ran at ground level but if a valley had to be crossed, rows of arches were built to keep the water at the right height. The Agua Marcia aqueduct had 7 miles (11 km) of arches. It was built in 140 B.C. to carry water a distance of 60 miles (91 km) above ground and underground to Rome. The two layers of arches of this aqueduct in Segovia, Spain, carried water 120 feet (36 m) above the streets.

Inside a town house

Most of our knowledge about Roman houses comes from archaeological discoveries at Pompeii and Herculaneum. Another find was Ostia, a port at the mouth of the Tiber River. Ostia had been buried under river mud for hundreds of years. Ash and mud protected these towns, and their buildings were well preserved. In Pompeii, archaeologists found houses with furniture, pots, and pans still in the rooms. There was even food on the table!

At first, the Romans built their houses of brick or stone. Later buildings were often made of concrete, decorated with brick or stone. They also used mortar to stick the bricks together.

▽ Most town houses had central heating. Hot air from a furnance passed through channels under the floor and up through pipes in the walls of the rooms. Some rich people also had a private bathroom.

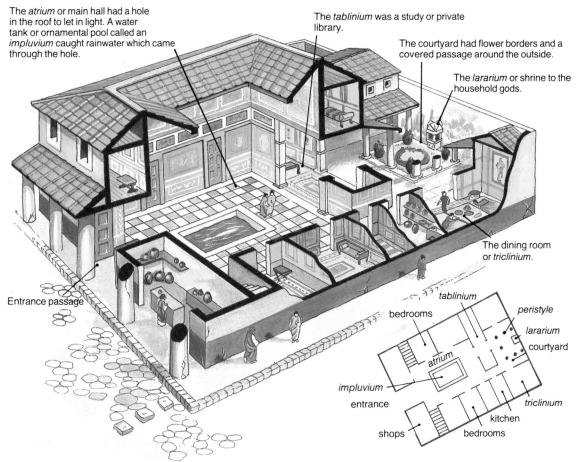

The *atrium* or main hall had a hole in the roof to let in light. A water tank or ornamental pool called an *impluvium* caught rainwater which came through the hole.

The *tablinium* was a study or private library.

The courtyard had flower borders and a covered passage around the outside.

The *lararium* or shrine to the household gods.

The dining room or *triclinium*.

Entrance passage

tablinium

bedrooms

peristyle

lararium

courtyard

impluvium

atrium

entrance

triclinium

kitchen

shops

bedrooms

◁ The poor people lived in a very different style. In Ostia and Rome they lived in blocks of apartments, sometimes with five or six floors. The rooms on the street level were often shops. There were also one-room schools and takeaway food shops in the blocks. People had to go down to fountains in the street for water. Shopkeepers and craftsmen lived above their shops. This street is in Herculaneum. Two families would have lived in the house, one on the upper floor the other on the ground floor. Some people had only one room.

Furniture and decoration

The Romans did not fill their rooms with much furniture. What they did have was made of wood, sometimes decorated with ivory or silver. Because wood rots quickly, very little Roman furniture still exists. Most of our evidence comes from wall paintings and other finds at Pompeii.

Roman houses contained beds, chairs, stools, and tables. At mealtimes, people lay on couches placed around three sides of a low table. Clothes, food, and books were stored in wooden cupboards and chests. Archaeologists have found lamps made of iron or pottery. Some lamps burned olive oil. Others had candles made of reeds coated with wax. Lamps and kitchen stoves were a fire risk and often set houses on fire.

△ Walls were decorated with paintings like this one, from a house near Pompeii. The woman is sitting on a chair made of bronze. Chairs were kept for women or honored guests. Everyone else sat on stools.

Cooking and eating

The Romans ate very simply until they got new ideas about food from conquered lands. Ovid writes that the first Romans did not have bread. They ate boiled meat and a sort of wheat broth, or thin soup.

The Romans copied many Greek ideas about food and how they ate it. The Greeks lay on couches for meals and invited guests to dinner. The Romans began to do the same. People ate with their fingers or with spoons. The Romans had knives but no forks. Petronius wrote that slaves brought bowls of water and towels for people to wash their hands during a meal. Slaves also served the meals.

The day began at dawn with a light breakfast of bread and cheese. The poet Martial wrote that he often had only a quick glass of water. Lunch was a

▽ Archaeologists have found examples of pottery and bronze cooking pots and pans all over the Roman empire. These discoveries made it possible to reconstruct this typical Roman kitchen. Rich people had large kitchens where servants cooked the food on charcoal stoves. Poor people often had no kitchen. They cooked on fires in the street or took their food to be heated in the large ovens of a baker's shop.

cold meal of bread, meat, and fruit. The main meal was dinner, which was eaten at about 4 o'clock in the afternoon. Sometimes guests were invited and the meal went on far into the night. Wine was drunk with all meals, often mixed with water or honey.

Some of our evidence about Roman food comes from the recipe book of Marcus Apicius, which was written in the 1st century A.D. The recipes give us details about the fruit, vegetables, meat, and fish the Romans ate and what herbs and spices they used to flavor their food.

△ A mosaic of seafood caught and eaten by the Romans. Many of them, like lobster, octopus, eel, and red mullet, are still found off the coasts of Italy.

Music and entertainment

On the day of a dinner party or feast, slaves were sent out to buy food from the shops. If the family did not have a cook, they hired one from the market where groups of slaves waited for jobs.

The feast had several courses, including shellfish, fish, wild boar, roast game birds, fruit, and sweets. Marcus Apicius gives recipes for cooking exotic meats such as peacock and ostrich. Many writers mention these feasts and remark that wealthy Romans ate far too much and spent too much money on their food. Between courses, the guests had serious conversations and discussions. There was usually some entertainment such as musicians, jugglers, dancers, and acrobats. Pliny wrote that he did not enjoy the entertainments much — he liked just talking better.

The people who played musical instruments at parties were often slaves. These musicians also played in the theaters and at sporting events. They played stringed instruments such as the harp and a type of lyre called the **cithara**. Wind instruments included the **pan pipes** and the trumpet. The guests never danced at parties. They thought it was beneath their dignity. They watched slave girls dance instead.

△ A mosaic found at Pompeii shows street entertainers playing music and dancing. The woman on the left is playing pan pipes and the man on the right is beating time on a tambourine. In the wall painting on page 33 the seated woman plays a cithara.

At the baths

Only rich people had baths in their own homes. Everyone else went to the public baths in the town. It was not expensive to go to the baths, and in some towns they were free. Most Romans, even the emperor, enjoyed going to the baths. People used them as a place for relaxation and to talk as well as to wash. Women could only use the baths at special times of the day, usually in the morning when the men were at work. In some places, there were separate baths for women.

There were over 900 public baths in Rome and many of them were enormous. The public baths built in Rome by the emperor Diocletian held 300 people. Men finished work at about 3:00 in the afternoon and went to the baths. They would spend about an hour there before going home for dinner. Before a bath, they would do some type of vigorous exercise. As well as the baths, there was a gymnasium and sports field where people could exercise or have a

◁ The Romans came to the English city of Bath. There they built a city much like one at home. This was the swimming pool of the Roman baths. It is still filled with water that flows along channels made by the Romans, from a nearby hot spring. People thought that the springwater cured sickness.

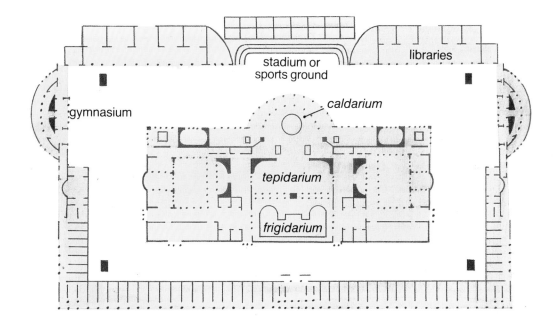

stadium or sports ground

libraries

gymnasium

caldarium

tepidarium

frigidarium

wrestling contest. There was also a swimming pool where both men and women could go. There were lounges, libraries, and restaurants where people could relax and meet friends after their bath.

Bathing and exercise kept the Romans fit and healthy, as well as clean. First the bather went to the *unctuarium* where a slave rubbed oil into his or her body. Then the bather went into the *tepidarium*, where there were two baths of warm water. Pliny tells us that one was big enough to swim in. Then the bather moved to a very hot bath called the *caldarium.* The room was filled with steam that made the bather sweat. This got rid of all dirt in the skin. The playwright Seneca did not enjoy the steamy room. "It's like being on a bonfire!" he said. The bather scraped the oil and dirt off his or her skin with a scraper called a strigil. Then the bather plunged into a cold bath called the *frigidarium* to close the pores of the skin. Finally a slave massaged the bather's body and rubbed scented oils into his or her skin, before the bather left the baths.

△ Several Roman baths are still standing, so we can see what they were like. The Caracalla Baths in Rome were built between A.D. 206 and 235. They were used by 1,600 bathers at a time until the invading Goths broke the aqueduct over 300 years later.

A public holiday

The Romans did not have weekends as we do today, but they had about 120 days of public holidays throughout the year. Many of these began as religious festivals. Some celebrations lasted for several days. On public holidays, the Romans went to the theater to watch plays or listen to concerts or poetry readings. They also went to the amphitheater or circus for chariot races or **gladiator** fights. Gladiators were slaves or criminals who were trained to fight. These professional fighters fought to the death to entertain the watching crowd.

Rich men who wanted to be elected to an important office used the religious holidays for "bread and circuses." They handed out free food and organized free chariot races or gladiator fights to win the support of the poor people.

Chariot races

Most towns had a circus or stadium where chariot races were held. Crowds of people came to watch the sport. The Circus Maximus in Rome held 250,000 people. Four teams of chariots took part in the races. The chariots were drawn by two or four horses and each team wore a different color — red, blue, green,

◁△ Gladiators wore armor and a helmet and fought with swords or a trident, which was a three-pronged spear. They often fought wild animals. The crowds enjoyed watching these fights to the death. At the games paid for by Emperor Trajan in A.D. 107, 11,000 wild animals were killed. At this amphitheater at El Djem in Tunisia, the animals were kept in underground cages. Sometimes the arena was flooded for mock sea battles between warships.

◁ Chariot racing was very dangerous. The drivers, or charioteers, were allowed to bump and ram each other and chariots were often knocked over. The charioteers wore helmets and leather chest and leg protectors. Even so, they were sometimes killed.

or white. The crowd bet on their favorite team and cheered them on as they raced. Each race was seven laps of the stadium, which was about 4 miles (6.5 km). The winning team won a money prize.

At the theater

Plays were performed in large open-air theaters, with the seats in a semicircle. The smallest theater in Rome had seats for over 7,000 people.

Roman actors wore large masks during a play because the audience was too far away to see the actors' faces. There were sad masks for tragedies and grinning masks for comedies.

Early Roman plays were translations of Greek comedies and tragedies. By the time of the empire in 27 B.C., writers began to produce plays based on Roman history. The most famous Roman writer of tragedies was Seneca, but Roman audiences preferred the comedies of Plautus and Terence who made up the phrase, "Where there's life, there's hope." Many Roman translations and plays survive today.

Crafts and trades

Greater wealth for some people brought problems for others. When Rome was first founded, most citizens worked for themselves. The plebeians of the republic were craftsmen and tradesmen as well as farmers. In 27 B.C., by the end of the republic, wealthy landowners had slaves to work on their large estates. The slaves took over many of the crafts and trades which the plebeians had done before. Now many plebeians were out of work. They went to the cities to find jobs, but few succeeded. There were craftsmen in the cities as well as on the big estates, but there was not nearly enough work for everyone.

City craftsmen

Craftsmen in the cities had their own workshops. They were helped by slaves and apprentices. Their goods were sold from their shops or in the market. Goldsmiths, silversmiths, and jewelers made luxury tableware, ornaments, and jewelry for the rich. Potters made clay plates, cups, and pots for use in the kitchen and for serving food on. Iron tools, weapons, and pots and pans for cooking were made by blacksmiths, while carpenters carved furniture and made other wooden items, such as picture frames and farm tools. There were also small factories where slaves spun and wove cloth. Cobblers made boots and sandals, and leatherworkers stitched belts and other leather goods, like shields for soldiers, from cowhide.

The poet Martial complained about the noise of the metalworkers in Rome. He said the bakers woke him up first, before dawn. Then all day there was the banging of the metalworkers' hammers. Metalworkers and jewelers needed metals and precious stones to work with. Precious stones such as amethysts and emeralds were imported from China and India. Gold and silver were mined in Spain and

△ Archaeologists have found many craftsmen's tools in excavations of workshops throughout the empire. They have found potters' workshops with kilns that show that pottery was fired as it is today. Potters made roofing tiles of baked clay as well as pots. Tiles have been found with the potter's name stamped on them. A workman scratched "I made 550 tiles" on a piece of Roman pottery found in England. Another worker had added "And I smashed 51." Both workers wrote in Latin. This shows where they were made. This wall painting from Pompeii shows a potter's workshop. A young apprentice is shaping a pot on the potter's wheel. The master potter looks on.

◁ Archaeologists have found Roman jars, bottles, bowls, and tumblers made of glass. Glass can be melted and used again, so these finds are rare. Romans learned the art of glass-blowing from Syria. Glass-blowing was invented in Syria in the 1st century B.C. before Syria became part of the Roman empire. Glass objects are difficult to make. Only rich people could afford these expensive things.

Macedonia. Iron was found in many areas, tin came from Britain and copper was mined in Italy, Cyprus, and Spain. The miners were slaves and their lives were very harsh. They often worked naked, though one carving shows them wearing aprons. The miners only had oil lamps to see by and they could hardly breathe in the airless, cramped conditions underground.

Shopkeepers

The forum was the main marketplace as well as the center of government. In the city of Rome there was a big market once a week as well as smaller markets near the forum. Many of these opened every day. They sold fruit and vegetables, meat, fish, and cloth. The streets around the forum were crowded with shops. There were butchers, bakers, grocers, barbers, booksellers, cloth sellers, oil sellers, and fullers. The fullers washed new woolen cloth to make it soft and thick. They also cleaned people's clothes. Stores were usually run by families with help from slaves. Street vendors sold food and drinks from roadside stalls.

Whole streets of shops have been found at Pompeii and Herculaneum. Each shop had a stone counter facing the street. At night, the shopkeeper pulled a wooden shutter down over the opening above the counter. At Pompeii, advertisements on the walls showed what each shop sold.

Buying and selling

Merchants and bankers had their offices in the forum. Merchants became rich by importing and exporting

◁ There are many stone carvings of stores that show us what they looked like and what they sold. This is a butcher's shop. You can see the butcher chopping a piece of meat while the customer sits waiting. Pieces of meat hang on hooks behind the butcher. In many shops, goods were laid out on a stone counter facing the street so that customers could look at them from outside. Roman women did not go shopping for food. Men did this job (or slaves in richer families).

goods, and bankers made their money from loans. People returning from foreign lands could also change money into Roman currency at a bank.

Many examples of Roman coins have been found all over the empire. There were gold *aurei*, silver *denarii*, and bronze or brass *sestertii*. One aurei was worth 25 denarii, and one denarii was worth four sestertii. The Romans weighed goods in libra, the Latin word for pound. A libra weighed 11½ oz (327 g). In A.D. 301 Emperor Diocletian published a list of prices. From this we know that a pound of beef or cheese cost eight denarii and eggs were one denarii each. A pheasant could cost 250 denarii. As an example of what this was worth, a carpenter earned 50 denarii a day and an elementary teacher earned 50 denarii a month for each pupil. Government inspectors called *aediles* visited markets and shops to check that food was correctly weighed and priced and that it was of good quality.

△ The pictures on Roman coins give interesting information. The head of the emperor was often shown on one side, like the head of the emperor Nero on this bronze sestertii. Achievements such as successful battles and the building of the Colosseum and the emperor Trajan's column in Rome were also shown.

◁ This bakery is one of many that have been found in Pompeii. On the right is the flour mill. Grain was poured into the upper part, which was turned by a slave. The stones ground the grain into flour. On the left is the oven. A fire was lit in the lower portion and the bread was baked in the upper part. When the loaves were cooked, the baker used a long metal pole with a flat part at one end to remove them. They were then laid out on the counter for sale.

Trade and transport

A rchaeologists have found Roman coins in many different countries. These coins are evidence of trade and travel. Pottery tells us more about where goods were made and sold, because potters often stamped their work with their own mark. Archaeologists can often match pieces of pottery with names found at sites of workshops far away. Oil, flour, wine, and other goods were carried in large pottery jars, called **amphorae.**

Underwater archaeologists find out more about trade and trade routes by studying wrecks of merchant ships. Archaeologists study the cargo and the ship itself. They piece together the evidence to see where the ship came from and where it was going. A few years ago, divers found a wreck of a Roman cargo ship off the coast of France. The amphorae still had wine inside.

Roman paintings and carvings show broad cargo

Trade in the empire

◁ Large merchant ships brought goods to the port of Ostia, at the mouth of the Tiber River. Porters unloaded the goods onto riverboats and men pulled the barges to warehouses along the banks of the Tiber. A new bigger port was built at Ostia in the time of the emperor Claudius. Recent excavations of the port of Ostia have revealed this mosaic of merchant ships and dolphins.

ships with sails and oars. The oars were used if there was no wind. Depending on the weather, a ship filled with cargo would take two to three weeks to sail from Egypt to Rome. The Romans traded throughout their empire for essential items like wheat but other luxury goods like silks, jewels, and spices came from as far away as China and India. The government controlled some imports and exports, but trade was also organized by private merchants. They could borrow money from a bank to buy cargo, although they risked everything if the ship was lost at sea.

It was cheaper to carry goods by sea than by land. Few Romans had horses, apart from the army, and carts or chariots pulled by oxen or mules were very slow. However, some people preferred to travel by land because of the risk of shipwreck or attack by pirates at sea. According to the writer Juvenal, travelers might meet bandits in some places, but most roads were safe. There were inns along main roads, where travelers could stay the night. Government officials could change horses at these inns. They rode fast, carrying messages from Rome to all parts of the empire. Ordinary people had to walk or ride mules or donkeys. In towns, people were sometimes carried in litters. A litter was a seat on long handles. It was carried by four or eight slaves. Curtains hid the person sitting in the litter.

△ A four-wheeled, horse-drawn cart used for carrying passengers. This stone carving was found in southern France.

Expansion and conquest

How did a small settlement on the south bank of the Tiber River grow into the center of a mighty empire?

By the 4th century B.C., Rome had defeated the Etruscans and established leadership over most of the other tribes to the south of Rome. In 391 B.C. the Gauls, invaders from the north, attacked Rome. The Romans bribed the Gauls with gold and they returned to their own lands. Now only one tribe was the enemy of Rome. This was the Samnite tribe who lived to the west of Rome. The Romans fought three bitter wars against the Samnites and defeated them in 290 B.C.

The Punic Wars

The Romans were now a strong force. They became interested in lands beyond their borders. This led to many years of war with the Carthaginians. These people came from the powerful and wealthy trading state of Carthage in North Africa. The Roman name for them was *Punicus,* which is why these wars are called the Punic Wars. The Romans and the Carthaginians first quarreled in 264 B.C., over the island of Sicily. They both wanted to control the island's ports and wheat fields. The Romans had to

◁ The Romans wanted to trade, but they were also determined to gain power at sea. To do this they had to build a fleet of warships. Each Roman ship could carry 400 soldiers. The ships had sails and oars. A new idea was a drawbridge with a spike. Roman ships always attacked the enemy from the side so they could dig the spike into the enemy ship. Then the Roman soldiers could cross the drawbridge onto the enemy ship and fight.

build a fleet of ships to fight at sea for the first time. They defeated the Carthaginians at Sicily in 241 B.C.

The Romans had only won the war at sea. Now the Carthaginian general, Hannibal, made a plan to attack Rome by land. The Romans did not expect an attack from the north because although the Carthaginians owned land in Spain it was a long way from Rome. Hannibal surprised the Romans by marching his army nearly 1,240 miles (2,000 km) and crossing two mountain ranges. In 218 B.C. Hannibal's army defeated the Romans at Trebbia in northern Italy. A Roman army was defeated again in 217 B.C., at Lake Trasimene in central Italy when Hannibal's army lay in wait in a narrow valley. They killed 70,000 Roman soldiers. The two sides met again the next year at Cannae in southern Italy. Again the Romans were defeated. Finally the Roman general, Scipio, decided to attack the Carthaginian colonies. He conquered Spain in 207 B.C. Then Scipio invaded North Africa. Hannibal went back to defend Carthage, but Scipio defeated Hannibal's army at Zama. Hannibal fled and later killed himself so he would not be captured.

△ This coin shows a portrait of Hannibal on one side and an elephant on the other. It may not be a good likeness but from the name on the coin we know it is Hannibal. Hannibal was very young when he became an army general but he nearly beat the Romans. Livy wrote: "He was the best among the foot and horse soldiers — first into battle and the last to leave."

Key
— → Hannibal's route
— → Scipio's invasion
✕ battles
☐ Roman territory
☐ Carthaginian territory

GAUL
The Alps
Trebbia ✕
218 B.C. ✕ Lake Trasimene
217 B.C.
The Pyrenees
Rome ●
✕ Cannae
216 B.C.
SPAIN
MEDITERRANEAN SEA
SICILY
● Carthage
✕ Zama
202 B.C.
NORTH AFRICA

The war with Carthage

◁ Hannibal marched for 5 months with his army of 60,000 men and 37 elephants. It took 15 days to cross the Alps and three quarters of his soldiers died. Hannibal had better horsemen than the Romans but his army was too small. He had hoped more people would join him as he marched toward Rome. The Gauls did, but the tribes the Romans had conquered stayed loyal to Rome. The Carthaginian colonies came under Roman rule in 202 B.C. The Romans finally conquered Carthage itself in 146 B.C.

Legionaries and centurions

The first Roman army was made up of ordinary citizens. Men between the ages of 17 and 60 had to serve in the army. The younger men might be called up to go away and fight in a war. Men of 46 or older did jobs like cleaning weapons and defending the city. Then, in 107 B.C., a fine soldier named Marius was chosen to be consul. He had served with the army in Spain. The Romans had also been fighting a long war at Numidia, in North Africa. Under the leadership of Marius, the Romans defeated the enemy. After this, Marius was made consul five more times.

Marius made changes to the army. He needed well-trained men who knew how to fight. Marius set up an army of volunteer soldiers. They had to join the army for 20 years as full-time soldiers. Many of the citizens did not like leaving their homes for months or even years to fight long wars. However, the soldiers were well paid, receiving about 225 denarii a year,

◁ **A standard-bearer**
Each legion had a standard, a pole with a silver eagle on top. The eagle was the emblem of Rome. The standard also had the emblem of the legion. The standard was carried by the standard-bearer, or *aquilifer*. In battle, the standard was raised or dipped to give orders to the soldiers in the rear.

△ **A legionary**
A legionary wore an iron helmet, a chain mail tunic over a wool tunic, and sandals on his feet. Later chain mail was replaced with a cuirass, that protected the shoulders and upper body. Below the cuirass the legionary wore a kilt that was made of strips of leather plated with metal.

He was armed with a short sword, a dagger, a shield, and a long spear.

and they were given land or money when they left the army. These professional soldiers were trained to march, fight, and build roads and bridges. The army was divided into regiments, or **legions**, of about 6,000 men. Each legion consisted of ten **cohorts**. In each cohort there were six **centuries**, or companies of 100 men. The ordinary soldiers were known as legionaries, and they were the foot soldiers. Each legion also had a troop of about 700 cavalry or soldiers who rode horses. A legionary could be promoted to a centurion, who commanded a century.

By the time of the empire, there were 28 legions. The soldiers lived in army camps or forts all over the empire. Each legion was commanded by a *legate.* He had six officers called *tribunes.* The senior tribune could take over command if necessary. The second most senior tribune was called the *prefect.* He was in charge of building projects.

△ Archaeologists have found many examples of Roman armor and weapons in Roman forts throughout the empire. Metal objects last a long time. They do not break apart and rot away if they are buried underground.

◁ **A centurion**
A centurion wore a more elaborate helmet and a cloak over his chain mail tunic. Sometimes the soldiers wore leg protectors, or greaves. In cold climates, they wore breeches.

At war

The large, well-equipped Roman army was trained to be an efficient fighting machine. Part of a soldier's training was to march with a pack weighing about 55 lb (25 kg) on his back. This prepared him for carrying all his own equipment, clothes, tent, food, and cooking pots when the army marched to war. The army marched about 20 miles (32 km) a day. When they came to a deep river, they built a pontoon bridge across it. To do this they made

△ There are many stone carvings of Roman battle scenes. Arches were built in Roman cities in memory of successful battles. Pictures carved on the stone sides tell the story of the battle. There are also scenes on tombs or the bases of statues of famous soldiers. The carvings show details of Roman weapons, armor, and battle techniques. Trajan's Column, in the forum in Rome, is carved with details of the emperor Trajan's wars with Dacia in A.D. 101 to 102 and 105 to 106. The carvings tell a continuous story in pictures which wind around the 100-foot (30 m) high column. About 2,500 figures are carved on the column.

◁ This picture of Roman soldiers using a battering ram was drawn long after Roman times by an artist who had studied their methods of siege warfare.

rafts of wood and tied them together so they reached from one side of the river to the other. Then the army crossed on this floating bridge. Each night they stopped and set up camp. This took several hours as they had to dig a ditch and make earth walls around the camp to protect their tents from attack.

The Jewish historian and soldier, Josephus, describes the Roman army marching into Galilee. Officers and standard-bearers were in front, followed by trumpeters. Then came the main army of legionaries, cavalry, and auxiliaries. At the back were the engineers and surveyors, doctors and priests. Slaves also went with the army to help with work like building roads.

The Romans were famous for their methods of **siege warfare** that they used to attack an enemy inside a fort or fortified town. Soldiers often used the **testudo**, or "tortoise," formation to approach the walls of the fort. They covered themselves with a "shell" of shields which could not be pierced by the enemy's arrows or spears.

Siege warfare

The Romans had several ingenious weapons for siege warfare. Imagine a town completely surrounded by high walls. On the walls are soldiers waiting to throw spears or fire arrows at approaching invaders. The Romans realized that they had to have some form of protection to get near the walls. They also had to have some weapons that were big enough to storm the walls or fire missiles from a distance.

The Romans used a mobile attack tower. Soldiers on the top could hurl spears into the town. As the tower approached the walls, a drawbridge was let down and the soldiers swarmed over the walls. Battering rams were used to break through the walls. The Romans also used a giant catapult called a *ballista* to hurl stones. Some could throw stones weighing about 88 lb (40 kg). Catapults were also used to fire arrows. The *ballista* is described in detail by Vitruvius. He was an architect and engineer for the army of Julius Caesar and of Augustus. From his description, historians have built this replica of a *ballista*.

Wars in Italy

The Romans were successful conquerors because of their army, but they had troubles at home. Quarrels between different groups of people led to wars in Italy, and even to **civil war**, when Roman citizens fought each other.

Italy had been a country of farmers. Each family had a small plot of land to grow food. As Rome became more powerful, the Romans took land from other tribes. The senate gave land to army leaders, as rewards for success in battles. Wealthy men also began to buy land and set up farms with slaves. Poor people had to move to the towns. Many plebeians were out of work. Rome was governed by a few wealthy men. There was discontent for many years. In 133 B.C. Tiberius was elected tribune to represent the plebeians. Tiberius made a plan to rent land to the poor, but wealthy men refused to give up any of their land. As a result, Tiberius and 300 of his supporters were murdered by the senators. His brother, Gaius Gracchus, was elected tribune ten years later. Gaius suggested the senate should buy wheat and sell it cheaply to poor people. He also thought all the people in Italy should be Roman citizens, not just the people of Rome. He was killed, too.

△ Pompey brought huge sums of money and treasures in gold and silver back to Rome from the lands he conquered. Pliny describes a procession through the city in 61 B.C. "There was also a portrait of Pompey made of pearls. It was pleasing with its swept-back hair and honest face."

Civil war

The senators were frightened by the unrest in Italy. They sent an army commanded by two generals, Marius and Sulla, to fight the rebels. Many people died and in 90 B.C., the senate promised to let all Italians be Roman citizens. Now Sulla and Marius became rivals. They each had the support of their soldiers and fought a civil war. Marius was an old man and died in 86 B.C. but fighting went on until 82 B.C. when Sulla won control of the senate. He retired in 79 B.C.

△ Julius Caesar had to gain the support of the people by becoming a brilliant conqueror like Pompey. This statue shows the type of armor warn by Roman generals.

◁ The story of Spartacus and the revolt of slaves against Rome is told in a ballet by Yuri Grigorovich, the director of a Russian ballet group. Spartacus was a slave. He escaped from the gladiator training school at Capua, in southern Italy, in 73 B.C. He led a group of other runaway slaves. They robbed and burned houses and fought battles. A senator called Sallust wrote a history of Spartacus and the 70,000 slaves who joined him in revolt. In 71 B.C. the senate asked Marcus Crassus to lead an army against the slaves. During the battle Spartacus was killed, and later thousands of his followers were crucified along the Appian Way.

The end of the republic

Sulla had shown that army generals could use the support of their soldiers to take power in Rome. In 70 B.C. two of Sulla's officers became consuls. One was Crassus, who ended the slaves' revolt. The other was Pompey, a brilliant and popular general.

In 59 B.C. Julius Caesar was elected consul. Then he became governor of southern Gaul. During the next nine years, Caesar brought northern Gaul under Roman rule as well. Pompey was jealous of Caesar and got the senate to order Caesar to resign his command. Caesar ignored the order and marched into Rome with his army. Pompey fled to Greece where Caesar defeated Pompey's army at Pharsalus in 48 B.C. Pompey escaped to Egypt where he was murdered.

In 46 B.C. Caesar returned to Rome in triumph. Dio Cassius tells us that the senate and the people granted him the title "father of his country." Caesar ruled Rome as a dictator. Some senators wanted to regain power for the senate. In 44 B.C., a group of senators stabbed Caesar to death in the senate house in the Forum Romanum.

The emperors

After Caesar's death, two men took over power. One was Caesar's great-nephew, Octavian, and the other his fellow consul, Mark Antony. Although Caesar's murderers had fled, Mark Antony tracked down the leaders, Cassius and Brutus, and killed them.

Octavian and Mark Antony began to struggle for power. They divided the empire between them. Octavian ruled over Italy and the west, and Antony took Egypt and the east. Antony was a stronger ruler than Octavian, but he fell in love with Cleopatra, the Queen of Egypt. He neglected his duties to stay at court with her, and Octavian became angry. In 31 B.C., Octavian declared war on Antony. His fleet met the fleets of Antony and Cleopatra near Actium on the west coast of Greece. Octavian defeated the enemy fleets, and Antony and Cleopatra killed themselves.

Octavian returned triumphant to Rome in 27 B.C. The senate gave him the power of *imperium* for 10 years. This meant he was the most powerful man in Rome. He could decide about the life or death of everyone. He could make laws and tell the senate when to meet. The word "emperor" comes from the Latin *imperium,* so when Octavian was given the

◁ The Arch of Titus stands in the Forum in Rome. It was built in memory of Titus who was emperor from A.D. 79 to 81. In A.D. 70 Titus commanded the Roman army that ended the Jewish revolt in Judaea. The arch celebrates the siege of Jerusalem and shows Roman soldiers carrying treasures from Jerusalem back to Rome.

The Roman emperors

Augustus 27 B.C. – A.D. 14 Augustus did not try to gain new lands for the empire because he thought it was big enough. He built many new roads to link the provinces in the empire. He chose governors for the provinces. He also arranged a system of paid officials to help the governors. Augustus was interested in the arts and encouraged writers such as Virgil and Livy.

The next four emperors were all related to Augustus. They became rulers because they were part of his family. They were not elected by the people. However they were not such good rulers as Augustus.

Tiberius A.D. 14 – 37 Tiberius was the stepson of Augustus. He strengthened the empire, but became a tyrant in his later years.

Caligula A.D. 37 – 41 Caligula continued the reign of terror. He was a great-grandson of Augustus. Caligula was probably mad. He made his horse a consul and had a special palace built for it!

Claudius A.D. 41 – 54 Claudius was Caligula's uncle. He began the Roman conquest of Britain.

Nero A.D. 54 – 68 Nero was Caligula's nephew and Claudius's stepson. He was a cruel and vain man. In A.D. 64, a great fire destroyed part of Rome. Nero blamed the Christians for starting the fire and had many of them killed. He saw himself as an artist and acted in the theater. His cruelty turned the people against him and he killed himself.

After Nero, the emperor was usually a general. The empire reached its greatest size in the reign of Trajan from A.D. 98 to 117. Trajan came from Spain and was the first emperor born outside Italy.

Emperor Augustus

power of *imperium* he also became the ruler of the whole empire. He also took the name Augustus. Augustus brought peace to the empire and under his rule Rome became a beautiful city.

During the republic, each consul could only serve for one year at a time. Augustus ruled as emperor until his death, in A.D. 14. He had already chosen the next emperor. At that time, the people of Rome could not elect their leader.

A Roman province

Augustus took control of the whole empire. He set up a new system to govern the provinces by appointing a governor for each one. They were men who had been consuls in Rome and commanders of legions in the Roman army. Each governor was in charge of a province for three to five years. He was paid a salary by the emperor and had other Roman officials to help him. The governor had to write reports to the emperor, collect **taxes** and hear legal cases. Soldiers lived in forts in the provinces to help keep control. The local people were only allowed to become Roman citizens after A.D. 211 when the emperor Caracalla made a new rule.

In A.D. 78 Julius Agricola was made governor of the Roman province of Britannia, or Britain. The writer Tacitus was married to Agricola's daughter. Tacitus's books describe in detail the conquest of this province and how the British people learned Roman customs and methods of doing things.

The conquest of Britain

Julius Caesar first invaded Britain in 55 B.C. Storms wrecked some of his ships and his cavalry could not

△ Hadrian's wall crossed Britain from east to west and was nearly 75 miles (120 km) long. It was built by Roman soldiers. Stone carvings record the names of the soldiers who built each part. The stone wall was over 19 feet (6 m) high and 10 feet (3 m) wide, with a deep ditch on the north side. Soldiers kept watch from towers and gate houses less than one mile apart. Housesteads is one of the 16 forts along the wall where the soldiers lived. About 14,000 soldiers were needed to guard the wall. Many parts of the wall can still be seen.

◁ In 1960 a workman digging a trench found some Roman pottery. This led to the discovery of the magnificent Roman palace at Fishbourne in England. Archaeologists have excavated many mosaic floors. The palace was large and must have belonged to a rich person. Marble on the walls came from Italy and Greece. The rooms were laid out around a courtyard garden, with hedges and fountains.

cross from Gaul or France. Caesar and his army left before the weather got worse. The next year he crossed the English Channel again. This time he had 800 ships, 25,000 soldiers and 2,000 cavalry. They won battles against the local tribes and made the people agree to send gifts to Rome. Caesar and his army returned to Rome before the winter.

The Romans did not invade Britain again until A.D. 43. Then the emperor Claudius conquered eastern and southern Britain. He called his son Britannicus in honor of his victory. The army commander, Aulus Plautius, became the first governor of the province. The Roman army continued to fight tribes to the north and the west. The second governor, Ostorius Scapula, defeated the British king, Caratacus, in Wales in A.D. 51. Tacitus writes that Caratacus fought bravely and told his Roman captors, "Because you wish to rule the world, does it follow that everyone will accept slavery?"

Life in Roman Britain

The British tribes lived in small wooden houses on hill-tops. The Romans showed them how to build homes of stone on lower ground, in towns with straight streets. Traders came to live by the forts to sell goods to the Roman soldiers. Temples, inns, and amphitheaters were built outside the walls. When the soldiers moved on, the workshops, hospitals, bath houses, and other fort buildings became part of the town. When they left the army, some soldiers stayed on in these towns and married British women.

Many British people began to learn Latin. Agricola set up schools with teachers from Rome and Greece. Tacitus tells us that wealthy people in Britain wore togas and had Roman furniture in their houses. Archaeologists have found the remains of Roman buildings in many parts of Britain.

△ The emperor Hadrian spent 15 years traveling around the Roman empire. He ordered the building of walls, ditches, and forts to protect the borders from invaders. In A.D. 122 he came to Britain with a new legion of Roman soldiers. Agricola had won battles and built roads and forts in Scotland. Then his soldiers were needed in other parts of the empire. Agricola's forts were abandoned. For many years tribes from Scotland attacked the Roman province of Britannia to the south. Hadrian decided to build a wall to keep them out.

The fall of Rome

The Romans ruled Britain for nearly 400 years. The cost of keeping soldiers in all the Roman provinces was very high. As more tribes attacked the borders of the empire, the emperors needed even more money for bigger armies. People did not want to pay higher taxes, and this led to unrest throughout the empire. The army divided and supported the claims of different men to be emperor. Between A.D. 211 and 284, twenty emperors were murdered. Civil war ruined trade and caused food shortages.

The government of the Roman empire was in chaos. In A.D. 284 the emperor Diocletian knew the empire had grown too big to govern properly. He divided it into 12 districts, each with its own governor. He chose his friend Maximian, to rule as emperor with him. When they retired, civil war began again until Constantine became emperor.

The last Roman emperor to rule in Italy was

△ This statue of the emperors Diocletian and Maximian now stands in the church of San Marco in Venice. The emperors are both in battle dress and stand together expressing their equal rule. Diocletian ruled over the eastern empire and Maximian ruled the western empire.

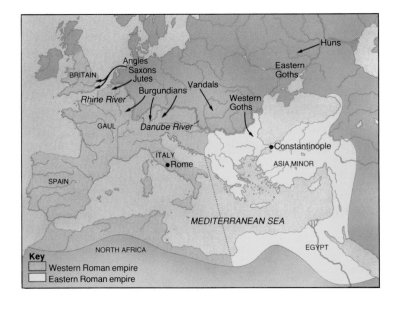

Key
Western Roman empire
Eastern Roman empire

◁ In A.D. 376 hordes of barbarians began to invade the empire. A hundred years later, the western empire had been divided into barbarian kingdoms. The Romans called all the tribes outside the Roman empire barbarians. This came from a Greek word for people who spoke foreign languages. In about A.D. 370 the German kingdoms beyond the Rhine and Danube rivers were attacked by a tribe from central Asia, called the Huns. The German tribes began to move west and south and invaded the Roman empire.

Romulus Augustus. He was defeated at Ravenna in A.D. 476 by a German named Odoacer. Italy became a German kingdom, with Odoacer as king.

The legacy of Rome

The barbarian invaders ransacked many Roman towns and left them in ruins. Roman traditions and customs and their building methods were forgotten. Many people still spoke Latin, however. It formed the basis of modern languages such as French, Spanish, and Italian. Rome also remained a center of Christianity, which Constantine had made the official religion of the whole empire.

In the 15th century a new age began. It was called the Renaissance, or rebirth. Scholars and artists began to rediscover the work of the Greeks and the Romans. They studied their art, literature, and architecture. The talents of these two civilizations have inspired people ever since.

△ Christianity helped the Roman empire and its traditions to survive. After Constantine became a Christian, he persuaded many people to follow his religion. After Constantine's death, Christian emperors continued to rule the eastern part of the Roman empire from Constantinople for another 1,000 years. In Rome the Pope became the most important figure. His priests began to spread Christianity throughout the barbarian tribes who took over the western part of the empire. Latin remained the official language of the Church for many centuries. Today the Pope is the head of the Roman Catholic Church and lives in the Vatican in Rome.

Time line

B.C.

753   The founding of Rome.

509   Tarquinius the Proud, the last king of Rome, is driven out. Rome becomes a Republic.

494   The plebeians are granted the right to choose their own tribunes.

391   The Gauls attack Rome and are bribed to leave.

367   The first plebeian consul elected.

290   The Romans defeat the Samnites.

264-241   The First Punic War with Carthage. The Romans build their first warships and learn to fight at sea.

218-201   The Second Punic War. Hannibal plans a surprise attack by marching, with 36 elephants, across the Alps.

149-146   The Third Punic War. Hannibal dies and Carthage is destroyed by the Romans. Rome becomes more powerful than ever, with North Africa as one of its provinces.

133   Tiberius Gracchus becomes tribune of the people.

123-122   Gaius Gracchus becomes tribune of the people.

107   Marius becomes consul and over the next few years sets up a new army.

91   The plebeians rebel against government.

82-80   Sulla rules Rome as a dictator.

73-71   The gladiator Spartacus leads a slaves' revolt. Spartacus is killed by the Roman army and the slaves' revolt is supressed.

58-49   Julius Caesar conquers Gaul and invades Britain twice.

49-45   Caesar defeats Pompey's army at Pharsalus. Pompey escapes to Egypt where he is murdered. Cleopatra is made queen of Egypt and Julius Caesar becomes the ruler of Rome.

44   Caesar is stabbed to death by Marcus Brutus.

43   Mark Antony and Octavian, Caesar's nephew, are in power.

42   Caesar's murderers Brutus and another senator, Cassius, are killed in Macedonia.

33-31   Octavian and Antony quarrel. Octavian defeats Antony at the Battle of Actium.

30   The death of Antony and Cleopatra.

27   Octavian becomes Augustus, the first emperor of Rome.

A.D.

14	Augustus dies and his stepson Tiberius becomes emperor.
14-37	Tiberius rules harshly, and then retires. Government in Rome goes into a decline.
37-41	Caligula becomes emperor on the death of Tiberius, but is murdered by his own guards.
41-54	Claudius, uncle of Caligula, becomes emperor.
43	Claudius invades Britain, adding the southern part of the island to the empire.
54-68	Claudius is poisoned by his wife, and her son Nero becomes emperor.
64	A great fire destroys most of Rome.
69-79	Nero dies and Vespasian becomes emperor.
79	The volcano Vesuvius erupts, causing the destruction of Pompeii and Herculaneum.
80	Emperor Titus opens the Colosseum in Rome.
98-117	Trajan becomes emperor.
101-105	The Dacian wars.
114	Trajan's column is built in Rome.
117-138	Hadrian becomes emperor.
122-126	Hadrian's wall built in northern Britain.
180-192	Commodus becomes emperor.
252	Barbarian tribes begin to invade the empire.

284-305	Diocletian becomes emperor.
306-337	Constantine becomes emperor.
313	Christianity becomes the official religion of the empire.
324-330	The new Christian capital of the empire is built at Constantinople, once Byzantium.
376	The barbarian invasions continue.
379-395	Theodosius becomes emperor.
395	The empire is officially divided into two halves.
410	The Goths make their first attack on the city of Rome.
445	The Vandals make a second attack on Rome.
476	The Gothic chief, Odoacer, defeats Romulus Augustus, the last emperor in the west, and declares himself king of Italy. The eastern empire continues to be ruled from Constantinople.

Glossary

abacus: a wooden frame with rows of sliding beads on wires, or in grooves, that is used for counting

amphitheater: an oval-shaped open building, with rows of seats around a central space where fights or games were held

amphora: a large two-handled clay storage jar used to transport cargo such as oil and wine. The amphora was also a Roman measure of volume, equal to 27 quarts (25.79 l)

apprentice: someone who learns a skill or trade by working with someone who is already expert at it. Apprentices worked for their teacher in return for their learning and were paid little or no money

aqueduct: a sloping bridge or channel, often built on arches, for carrying water overland. The Romans built aqueducts to supply their towns with water

archaeologist: a person who tries to work out what happened in the past by finding and studying old buildings and objects

augur: a religious person, employed by the Roman government, who looked into the future by studying the actions of birds

century: a Roman company of 100 soldiers, led by a centurion

cithara: a small hand-held stringed musical instrument which is played with a small pointed piece of bone or ivory

citizen: somebody who lives in a city and is allowed to take part in choosing its rulers

civil war: a war between people of the same country, rather than between different countries

civilization: a large group of people who have settled in one place and who live in the same way. They have rules and laws

cohort: a division of the Roman army consisting of six centuries, or 600 men

colony: a group of people who settle away from their own country, or land, but still consider themselves to belong to it

concrete: a strong building material made from a mixture of cement, water, sand, and broken stones. Cement is made from limestone

conquer: to overpower or defeat something, usually a country

consul: the title of the two chief magistrates or officials in Rome. Consuls, elected to serve for one year, were in charge of law and order and the armies of Rome

cult: a type of worship or religious belief. The word *cult* comes from the Latin *cultus* meaning "worship"

democracy: a country, or part of a country, that is ruled by a government chosen by all its citizens

dictator: a ruler who has complete power over a country or empire. Dictators usually take power by force and keep it by making people afraid of them

elected: to be chosen by the people in an election

emperor: the overall ruler of an empire. Augustus was the first Roman emperor

empire: a group of countries that are all under the rule of one country. An empire is ruled by an emperor

excavate: to remove layers of earth to uncover the remains of buildings

forum: a public place or meeting. In Roman towns the forum was both the marketplace and a meeting place

gladiator: a slave trained to fight at a special gladiatorial school. Gladiators fought each other or wild animals such as lions, tigers, and bears

inscription: something written or cut into another material like stone or paper

invader: someone who enters without permission. Invaders usually enter a country in large numbers in order to attack it

legion: the largest division in the Roman army. It consisted of 4,000 to 6,000 foot soldiers and cavalry and was led by a legate

magistrate: a person whose job it is to create laws and make sure they are carried out. Rome was ruled by a number of different types of magistrates, of which the two consuls were the most powerful

oratory: the art of speaking well in public. A good orator can speak about something without reading from notes, and without getting confused or taking too long

pan pipes: a musical instrument made from hollow reeds or pipes that are fixed together with their mouthpiece in line. Different notes are played by blowing into different pipes

patrician: a rich Roman citizen. Patricians were often landowners

philosopher: a person who studies philosophy, or the meaning of life and the way people behave

plebeian: any Roman citizen who was not a member of the wealthy patrician class. Plebeians were farmers, traders, and servants

province: a division or part of a country or an empire. Each Roman province was ruled by a governor

republic: a country or group of countries where the government is elected or chosen by the people. The word comes from the Latin *res publica*, which means the concern of the people

senate: the group of about 300 Romans who advised the magistrates. The word comes from the Latin *senex* meaning "an old man"

shrine: a place or structure which is thought to be holy or of religious importance

siege warfare: the constant attack by one army on the fortified position of another until they are forced to give in

stola: a long, loose outer robe worn by Roman women. Like togas, the stola was usually made of woolen cloth

stylus: a pointed tool used to make marks in soft materials like clay or wax. The Romans used a stylus to write on wax tablets

tax: a payment made by the people of a country, or an empire, to their government. Taxes pay for the running of a government and all that it provides

testudo: a protective covering of overlapping shields used by Roman soldiers to protect themselves as they approached the walls of an enemy town. The word comes from the Latin *testudinis* meaning "tortoise shell"

toga: a loose outer garment worn by citizens of Rome. Togas were usually made of a long woolen sheet

tribune: an official who represented the plebeians in the government

underworld: a place where the spirits of the dead went. The ancient Greeks believed in the underworld and the Romans adopted many of their gods and beliefs

Index

Agricola, Julius 56, 57
amphitheater 6, 38, 57
Andronicus, Livius 18
Antony, Mark 54
Apicius, Marcus 35
aqueducts 29
archaeology 6, 7, 8, 14, 24, 25, 28, 32, 33, 44, 57
army 26, 46, 47, 48, 49, 50, 51, 52, 53, 54, 56, 57, 58
astrologers 22
Augustus 5, 21, 28

barbarian invaders 59
baths 30, 36, 37
"bread and circuses" 38, 52
Britain 20, 25, 28, 56, 57, 58
building materials 30, 32
building techniques 4, 5, 30, 31, 57, 59

Caesar, Julius 5, 11, 53, 54, 56, 57
Carthage 46, 47
Cato 18, 27
chariot racing 38, 39
children 14, 17, 18
Cicero 13, 16, 22, 23
citizens 10, 12, 13, 14, 29, 40, 48, 52, 56
civil war 52, 54, 58
Claudius 57
Cleopatra 54
Columella, Lucius 25
Constantine 21, 58, 59
conquests 5, 18, 20, 25, 26, 29, 46, 47, 52, 56
craftsmen 40
Crassus 53
crops 25

Dio Cassius 53
Diocletian 36, 43, 58
divorce 17

education 18, 19, 57
elections 8, 10, 11, 38
emperors 5, 11, 21, 55, 56, 58
empire, the 5, 21, 25, 28, 39, 43, 45, 49, 54, 55, 58, 59
employment 40, 52
entertainment 35
Etruscans 4, 46
exports 26, 43, 45

farming 4, 24, 25, 26, 27, 40, 52
feasts 16, 35
festivals 21, 22, 26, 38
food 24, 26, 34, 35, 43
forts 29, 49, 51, 56, 57
forum, the 10, 13, 42
France 25, 28, 44, 57
furniture 32, 33, 40, 57

Gauls 46, 53
gladiators 38
gods and goddesses 16, 20, 21, 22, 23, 26
government 10, 11, 12, 42, 45, 52, 56, 58
governors 11, 13, 53, 56, 57
Greek influences 18, 19, 20, 21, 23, 29, 34, 39, 57, 59

hairstyles 15
Hannibal 47
Herculaneum 6, 7, 32, 42
holidays 38
Homer 18
houses 28, 32, 33, 57

imports 26, 42, 45

Josephus 51
Justinian 13
Juvenal 45

language 4, 5, 59
Latin 4, 5, 9, 10, 16, 18, 57, 59
laws 5, 10, 12, 13, 54
life-style 6, 8, 16, 17, 34, 35, 36, 37
lighting 33
Livy 8

magistrates 10, 11, 12, 13
Marius 48, 52
markets 35, 42, 43
marriage 16, 17
medicine 23
mining 26, 40, 41
money 43, 58
music 35

Octavian (Augustus) 54, 55, 56
Ovid 34

patricians 12
Petronius 34
philosophers 18

Plautus 17, 39
plebeians 12, 13, 40, 52
Pliny 8, 17, 22, 23, 35, 37
Pompeii 6, 7, 8, 32, 42
Pompey 53
provinces 11, 56, 58
Punic Wars, the 46

religion 20, 21, 38, 59
republic, the 4, 5, 10, 40, 55
roads 31
Roman calendar 27
Roman numerals 19
Rome 4, 5, 10, 12, 13, 18, 24, 26, 30, 36, 38, 40, 42, 46, 47, 52, 53, 54, 55, 57, 58, 59
Romulus, Augustus 58, 59
rulers 5, 11, 53, 55, 58

Samnites 46
senate, the 11, 12, 13, 21, 52, 53, 54
ships 44, 45, 47, 56, 57
Sicily 13, 26, 47
siege warfare 51
slaves 10, 16, 18, 24, 25, 27, 34, 35, 37, 38, 40, 41, 51
  revolt 53
soldiers 20, 29, 47, 48, 49, 52, 53, 56, 57, 58
sport 38, 39
stores 28, 35, 42
Sulla 52, 53

Tacitus 8, 22, 56, 57
Tarquinius the Proud 4
taxes 56, 58
teachers 18, 19, 57
temples 22, 57
theaters 38, 39
Tiber River 4, 32, 46
togas 14, 57
towns 28, 29, 36, 38, 45, 57, 59
  planning 29
trade 4, 40, 42, 43, 44, 45, 57, 58

Vesuvius, Mount 6, 8
Virgil 25
Vitruvius 30

wars 24, 46, 47, 48, 51, 54
women 10, 14, 17, 36
writers 8, 17, 18, 24, 30, 34, 35, 39, 45, 46